— P E O P L E   T O   K N O W —

BILL CLINTON

United States President

Michael D. Cole

ENSLOW PUBLISHERS, INC.

Bloy St. and Ramsey Ave. P.O. Box 38
Box 777 Aldershot
Hillside, N.J. 07205 Hants GU12 6BP
U.S.A. U.K.

Library of Congress Cataloging-in-Publication Data

Cole, Michael D.
    Bill Clinton: United States president / Michael D. Cole.
        p. cm. — (People to know)
    Includes bibliographical references (p.) and index.
    ISBN 0-89490-437-X
    1. Clinton, Bill, 1946- —Juvenile literature. 2. Presidents—United
States—Biography—Juvenile literature. [1. Clinton, Bill, 1946- . 2. Presidents.]
I. Title. II. Series.
E886.C65 1994
973.929'092—dc20   93-37411
[B]   CIP
                                                                 AC
Printed in the United States of America

10 9 8 7 6 5 4 3 2 1

Illustration Credits: AP/Wide World Photos, pp. 4, 94, 96, 100; *Arkansas
Democrat-Gazette,* pp. 21, 23, 24, 31, 52, 58, 63, 67, 69, 71, 75, 79;
Clinton/Gore Campaign, p. 89.

Cover Illustration: AP/Wide World Photos

Contents

With daughter Chelsea at his side and wife Hillary holding the Bible, Bill Clinton was sworn in as the 42nd President of the United States in Washington D.C. on January 20, 1993.

1

William Jefferson Clinton

Many years ago, when the young boy first placed his hands around his grandmother's gift of a new Bible, neither he nor his family in that small Arkansas town ever dreamed it would be used as it was used on January 20, 1993. That day, on the steps of the U.S. Capitol, before a throng of thousands of people and millions of television viewers around the world, the man placed his left hand on that same Bible, raised his right hand, and repeated a solemn oath administered to him by the Chief Justice of the United States:

"I, William Jefferson Clinton, do solemnly swear . . . that I will faithfully execute the office of President of the United States . . . and will to the best of my ability . . . preserve, protect, and defend the Constitution of the United States."[1]

Bill Clinton's wife Hillary held the Bible for him,

5

and his twelve-year-old daughter Chelsea stood at his side. January 20, 1993, was an unseasonably warm and brilliantly sunny day in Washington, D.C. With the oath of office completed, the Chief Justice reached across the Bible and firmly shook the hand of the new President of the United States, William Jefferson Clinton. Cheers and wild applause rose from the crowd and the band nearby played "Hail to the Chief" for the new President for the first time.

Bill Clinton, the long-time governor of Arkansas who had defeated incumbent President George Bush by convincing voters that America needed to be set on a new course, was now President Clinton. As President, he now had to set that course while dealing with a difficult set of problems in a changing world.

"Profound and powerful forces are shaking and remaking our world, and the urgent question of our time is whether we can make change our friend and not our enemy," he said in his inaugural address.

"When most people are working harder for less; when others cannot work at all; when the cost of health care devastates families and threatens to bankrupt our enterprises great and small . . . we have not made change our friend.

"Though our challenges are fearsome, so are our strengths," he continued. "There is nothing wrong with America that cannot be cured by what is right with America."[2]

Bill Clinton saw his presidency as a time of change. He was the first "baby boomer" President—the first President born after World War II. And he had come of age during the upheavals of the 1960s. For these and many other reasons, his approach to government was different than that of George Bush and Ronald Reagan before him.

"We must invest more in our own people," he said at his inauguration, "in their jobs and in their future, and at the same time cut our massive debt. And we must do so in a world in which we must compete for every opportunity.

"It will not be easy; it will require sacrifice. But it can be done and done fairly, not choosing sacrifice for its own sake, but for our own sake."[3]

If America was truly at a crossroads and in need of reinventing itself for what he called a "season of American renewal," Clinton seemed uniquely qualified to lead the way. For the young boy from a small and poor town in Arkansas to become President of the United States, it had been essential for him to reinvent himself many times. From humble beginnings, he had come a long way along an often bumpy path.

Now the American voters had elected him to chart a new path for the country into a future full of uncertainties, and he had already warned that that path "will not be easy."

After the ceremony, Clinton stood on the east side of

the Capitol Building and waved to the now former President Bush, who then stepped into a helicopter and was flown out across the Potomac River to a jet waiting to take him home to Houston. The challenges of governing were now officially shifted onto Bill Clinton's shoulders.

The American people were waiting to see what he could do. Most of all they were hoping. They hoped he could now deliver on his plans to create jobs, reform the health care system, train the work force of the future, and cut the rapidly growing federal deficit.

He and the country also faced the problems of many environmental concerns, the need for reform in our schools, the AIDS crisis, the ongoing debate over abortion, the question of gays in the military, and whether or not to become involved in an ugly war between Serbs and Muslims in Bosnia. And he faced all these challenges with the prospect of working with a Congress that was endlessly bickering.

The country wanted results, and many Americans hoped that this President—who had made so many promises to change things—would deliver on his promises. But could he? Should he? Although 43 percent of the voters elected him, were Congress and the American people ready for his programs?

"We can seize this moment," he said in his speech to the Democratic National Convention in July 1992. "We can make it exciting and energizing and heroic to be an

American again. We can renew our faith in ourselves and each other, and restore our sense of unity and community."[4]

The close-knit community Bill Clinton grew up in helped him through the challenges of his youth and shaped him into who and what he was. Clinton thought the government should play a larger role in helping American communities provide a better quality of life for their citizens. He believed a renewed sense of community was as important to the future of America as it had been in his own life.

"I end tonight where it all began for me: I still believe in a place called Hope."[5]

2

Hope, Arkansas

Near the southwestern corner of Arkansas, where Arkansas borders Texas and Louisiana, lies the little rural farm community of Hope. In the years after World War II, the late 1940s, Hope was a quiet, friendly community full of hard-working people. It was an All-American small town in many ways, but Bill Clinton was not born into a storybook family.

Clinton's father, William Jefferson Blythe III, was working as a traveling heavy equipment salesman based out of Chicago, while his wife, Virginia, was pregnant with their first child. Blythe made frequent trips back to Hope to visit Virginia, who was then living with her parents until Blythe could set up a permanent residence in Chicago and move them there.

When Virginia was six months pregnant with Bill,

Blythe drove to Arkansas intending finally to bring her back to Chicago and start their new family life. Blythe headed down Highway 61, but he never made it home. His car blew a tire and went off the road; he was knocked unconscious and thrown face down into a drainage ditch. He sustained only a small bruise on his head, but the unconscious William Blythe drowned in water only a few inches deep.[1]

William Jefferson Blythe IV was born three months later on August 19, 1946. Soon family members were calling him "Bill" and "Billy" as they had called his father. Although Virginia was happy with her new son, she still mourned her husband's death and knew that her and Billy's hardships were far from over.[2] When he was only two years old, Virginia had to leave Bill in Hope with his grandparents. She wanted to become a nurse-anesthetist and the nearest training facility was hundreds of miles south in New Orleans. Virginia visited when she could, but the young mother and her little son endured many long separations.

Bill stayed in Hope with his grandparents, Eldridge and Edith Cassidy, who owned a small grocery store in the black section of town. Clinton remembers that his grandfather extended credit to poor families in the town to make sure they had food on the table, and that he did so whether the families were white or black—a gesture that was not so common in the South in the 1940s and

1950s, and a lesson in kindness that was not lost on young Bill.

His grandparents also planted in him the first seeds of a strong belief in education. Clinton said his grandparents "taught me to count and read. I was reading little books when I was three. They didn't have much formal education, but they really helped embed in me a real sense of educational achievement, which was reinforced at home."[3]

When Bill was four, his mother returned from her training in New Orleans. Back in Hope, she met a local car dealer named Roger Clinton. They were married in 1950, and in 1954 they moved to Hot Springs where Roger worked at a Buick dealership and Virginia worked as a nurse-anesthetist at a local hospital.

Hot Springs was an exotic place compared to the tiny town of Hope. The town's base population of several thousand had swelled with travelers from all over the country because the town had wide-open gambling—with casinos and slot machines everywhere. It was all illegal, but state and local officials had always looked the other way. The gambling was so wide open that it never occurred to Virginia that it was illegal, until a new governor ordered the gambling shut down in 1967. "I never was so shocked," she said.[4]

When he was in the first grade, Bill attended public school in Hope, but when the family moved to Hot Springs, Virginia put her second-grader in a Catholic school, St. John's, even though the family were devout Southern Baptists. Virginia thought the smaller Catholic school would provide a smoother transition for Bill to the much larger public schools in Hot Springs.

Bill got good grades at St. John's, but one time a nun sent home Bill's report card with a low mark in conduct. The nun told Virginia there was really no problem, but because he was so sharp and alert and knew all the answers, he was not giving the other children a chance to answer. She had to get his attention somehow, and this was the only way she knew to do it. Bill got the message and learned to give his classmates an equal chance.[5] Two years later, when Bill was nine, Virginia switched him from St. John's to Ramble Elementary, a public school.

Bill was already reading the newspaper and becoming very interested in current events. By the time the family bought its first black-and-white television set in 1955, Bill was fascinated with the political news, especially the 1956 Democratic National Convention.

"I think it sort of came home to me in a way on television that it wouldn't have otherwise," Clinton later said. He watched with a sense of immediacy the fight between John F. Kennedy and Estes Kefauver for the vice-presidential nomination in 1956; this left a lasting impression on the youngster.[6] Kefauver went on to win the nomination, but the ticket he shared with Adlai

Stevenson lost to incumbent President Dwight Eisenhower and Vice President Richard Nixon.

Bill was popular at school and was known for saying "Hot Dog!" whenever he got excited. He and his friends played a lot of touch football and Monopoly, and listened to Elvis Presley records until they had most of them memorized. Clinton's childhood friends remember that he was considerate of them and kind to other people. One of his friends, David Leopoulos, remembers one Thanksgiving when Bill's mother sent him to get a loaf of bread from the grocery store. Bill saw a young boy sitting alone at the bus stop there.

"This person had a bag of potato chips in his hand," Leopolous said. "Bill noticed that he didn't seem very happy, so he went up and introduced himself to the boy."[7] Bill soon learned that the boy wasn't having any Thanksgiving dinner that day. A while later Bill brought the boy tramping through Virginia's back door to eat Thanksgiving dinner with them.

When Bill was ten, his mother and stepfather had a son whom they named Roger Clinton, Jr. Bill spent a great deal of time, especially while he was a teenager, taking care of his younger brother when his mother and stepfather were at work. He developed an almost fatherly relationship with young Roger. Bill's mother often left for work before the boys were awake, so Bill had to get his younger brother out of bed, get him dressed, and off to school.

Clinton's friend John Criner remembers Bill Clinton showing this kind of responsibility and independence at an even earlier age. "I can remember Bill Clinton's mother taking him to the hospital in the middle of the night when she'd have to go do a case, and she'd wrap him up asleep . . . take him in the hospital, and he'd sleep there. I can remember Bill as a kid going to Park Place Baptist Church, and he'd walk down the street every Sunday morning going to church by himself."[8]

Although the work of his mother and stepfather provided a home and the essentials of a comfortable life for Bill and his family, all was not well at the Clinton home. Roger Clinton's drinking habits had turned him into an alcoholic. When he drank too much, he would frequently become angry and violent, sometimes toward Virginia. Roger and Virginia had several brief separations during which Virginia would take the children and stay with someone for a short time. But the couple would eventually get back together again.

One night Roger fired a gun in the house. Virginia gathered up Bill and Roger, Jr. and left. "Roger spent that night in jail," Virginia said.[9] But they were soon back together.

The challenges Bill encountered during this turmoil at home may account for some of the pressure he put on himself at a young age, the seeking to put more order in his life. The unusual maturity and sense of responsibility fostered by these experiences began to show themselves even more as he attended Hot Springs High School.

"Bill was forced into an independence early, which I think has a bearing on his leadership," said Carolyn Staley,[10] one of Clinton's closest high school friends. She spoke of Bill's competitive nature and his drive to succeed in school.

"He had to be the class leader," she said. "He had to be the best in the band. He had to be the best in his class, in grades. And he wanted to be the top in anything that put him in the forefront of any course.[11]

Clinton was a leader of many clubs and organizations in high school, but he didn't win everything. He ran for senior class secretary, telling his opponent, "If you beat me, I'll never forgive you." He lost—to his friend Carolyn Staley—but she remains one of his very close friends today.[12]

Bill lost that race, but from the beginning of his high school years it had been clear that whatever Bill Clinton chose to do, he was going to try to be the best at it. He still faced some difficult problems at home, but he was very bright, and not afraid to work.

He was growing up in a hurry.

3

Growing Up in a Hurry

It seemed that Bill Clinton was always busy during high school. He set high goals for himself and was always highly motivated to achieve them, and in a hurry.

The fact that he had a father he never knew, a father who had died so young, spurred Bill on to realize his goals in a hurry. "I think I always felt, in some sense, that I should be in a hurry in life, because it [his father's death] gave me a real sense of mortality . . . most kids never have to think about when they're going to run out of time, when they might die. I thought about it all the time because my father died at twenty-nine, before I was born . . . . I think it's one reason I was always in such a hurry to do things.

"And I also think I thought I had to live for myself and for him too," he continued. "It's a funny thing, but the older I get the more I realize that sort of shaped my childhood."[1]

As a teenager, Bill worked part-time at a hospital and was active in DeMolay, a civic organization for young people. Many local civic groups sought out Bill to chair their fund-raising drive and campaigns in the community. So many organizations were recruiting Bill that his high school principal had to put a stop to it—his activities with the organizations were causing him to miss too much school.[2]

There was no doubt that Bill Clinton was very bright, and he was successful in school. But the reputation he gained in the community can be attributed to the force of his personality.

"He was . . . generous with his time, helping newcomers to Hot Springs High," classmate Glenda Cooper remembers. "I was struck by his positive attitude, his intelligence, and his sincerity. He seemed so comfortable with himself, his abilities, and he was so optimistic about the future. I remember thinking that he was a great campaigner, so energetic, compassionate, funny, talented and involved."[3]

"Bill would walk into my house when we had relatives or friends visiting from out of town," Carolyn Staley recalls, "and by the time he left they were marveling at this young man. He had such a natural gift for conversation, was impressive and charismatic, and made a lasting impression."[4]

The young Bill Clinton, the standout student at Hot Springs High, was the picture of a fine young man, filled with the civic-minded idealism of the early 1960s. But Bill's life was far from perfect. His stepfather's drinking problem continued, as did the fighting and the host of other family problems that sprang from Roger's alcoholism. One night, when he was fourteen and now grown to the same height as his stepfather, Bill brought part of the problem to an end.

Roger had been fighting with Bill's mother and his younger brother. Bill couldn't bear it anymore and decided to put a stop to it. "I just broke down the door of their room one night when they were having an encounter," Clinton said, "and told him that I was bigger than him now, and there would never be any more of this while I was there."[5] Bill grabbed Virginia and his brother and told his stepfather: "You will never hit either of them again. If you want them, you'll have to go through me."[6]

Roger Clinton stopped hitting them, but he and Virginia were divorced that same year. But a year later, despite Bill's efforts to dissuade his mother, they remarried. Although he had his doubts about its success, Bill very much wanted his mother's marriage to work. People had been calling him Bill Clinton for years. In a gesture to show support for his mother after the remarriage, when Bill was sixteen years old, he had his last name legally changed from Blythe to Clinton. He hoped it might help give the family some of the unity it so badly needed.

Amid his busy schedule at school and his unpredictable home life, Bill found time and energy to devote to music. He became a talented musician on the saxophone, making it into the All-State band on tenor sax. Bill also played in a jazz trio with friends Randy Goodrum and Joe Newman. They wore dark glasses in order to look like true jazz musicians, calling themselves the "Three Blind Mice." One day Governor Bill Clinton would play his saxophone on *The Tonight Show,* and later during his presidential campaign on *The Arsenio Hall Show.*

Clinton considers his experiences with music and the high school band some of the most important experiences of his youth. "Music, to me was—is, kind of representative of everything I like most in life," he said. "It's beautiful and fun, but very rigorous. If you wanted to be good, you had to work like crazy. And it was a real relationship between effort and reward. My musical life experiences were just as important to me, in terms of forming my development, as my political experiences or my academic life."[7]

Bill Clinton's talents and abilities were taking shape during his high school years. At the same time, he began thinking about what he might like to do in the future.

"When I was 16, I decided if I had a chance I would go into politics," Clinton said. "I had been interested in

By the time he was a senior in high school, Bill had become a talented tenor saxophonist. He even once thought about a career as a musician. Here he is playing in his high school orchestra. He also played in a local jazz trio called the "Three Blind Mice."

being a musician, a physician, or a politician. While I was very good at music, I would never be great. In politics, I thought I had unique abilities—I was genuinely interested in people and in solving problems. It was something I could be good at. Something I could love."[8]

Perhaps his most important political experience in high school was being elected a delegate to Boys' Nation, the civics program run by the American Legion to teach young leaders about politics, government, and the electoral process. Bill was elected to go to the national convention, which meant a trip to Washington, D.C., where he and the other delegates would walk the same halls as did the nation's power elite. He attended Boys' Nation in July of 1963, the summer before his senior year of high school.

During the visit, Bill ate lunch in the Senate Dining Room with Arkansas Senator J. William Fulbright, a man whom Clinton admired for his expertise in foreign affairs during years of service on the House and Senate Foreign Relations committees.[9]

The group was also invited to a tour of the White House. They were all ecstatic when President John F. Kennedy emerged to greet them in the Rose Garden.[10] Bill, like many young people at that time, idolized John Kennedy. During the brief visit, Bill stepped forward to express his admiration and shake President Kennedy's

A big moment for Bill Clinton. While visiting Washington D.C. as a delegate to Boys' Nation in July 1963, Clinton met and shook hands with President John F. Kennedy, a man whom Bill greatly admired.

Bill Clinton as a senior at Hot Springs High School.

hand. This was a big moment in Bill Clinton's young life.

Clinton's mother remembers the day he returned home from Boys' Nation. "When he came back from Washington, holding this picture of himself with Jack Kennedy, and the expression on his face, I knew right then that politics was the answer for him."[11]

On November 22, 1963, only four months after Bill had shaken his hand in the Rose Garden, President Kennedy was assassinated in Dallas. Kennedy had instilled a sense of hope and idealism in many young Americans in the early 1960s. His sudden death, and the growing problems over the war in Vietnam, began a slide for the country into pessimism and mistrust of the government and its institutions, and marked the beginning of an era of turmoil.

Bill Clinton would be entering college soon, determined to become a politician someday. But he would come of age during an era of hard choices and division—an era of conflict unlike that of any faced by his elders. The choices he and other young people would make during these difficult years would have a lasting affect on him, his generation, and the country.

4

A Sixties Education

"I often joke with my friends that on balance I'm still glad I was a child of the 60s," Clinton has said, "but there sure was a price to pay, if nothing else in the way people look back at us, like the marijuana thing."[1]

Clinton refers to a common image of youth in the 1960s—an image of long-haired hippies wearing tattered clothes, smoking marijuana, listening to loud rock music, and protesting the Vietnam War or burning their draft cards. It is a powerful image that lingers in the mind, but it did not exactly fit all young people attending college in the 1960s, including Bill Clinton. But while Clinton rarely reflected those images of the time, he reflected many of the ideas.

As he began attending Georgetown University in Washington, D.C. in 1964, he would be in the thick of how these ideas affected the country. It was very difficult at that time for a Southerner to get into the prestigious school, but Clinton's long list of accomplishments had given him the credentials he needed to be accepted into Georgetown's international studies program.

The young man from Arkansas hit the ground running at Georgetown, being elected class president in his freshman and sophomore years. Running for class offices wasn't considered stylish at Georgetown at that time, but Clinton's charm and personality seemed to disarm everyone he met.

College friend Dru Bachman remembers Clinton's attitude at Georgetown. "He openly admitted to being a small-town boy who had come to the big city to soak up every ounce of information and experience he could find," Bachman said, "and he proceeded to do just that with a hunger and gusto bewildering to those with far less self-assurance."[2]

Clinton described Georgetown as "an incredible experience . . . like a feast . . . . I'd never been out of Arkansas really very much, and there I was with people from all over the country and all over the world . . . teachers from all over the world."[3]

The school was expensive so, like many college students, Clinton had to work part-time jobs to bring in extra money. During his first summer off, he worked back in Arkansas on a campaign to elect a man named Frank Holt governor. Holt lost, but during the campaign

Clinton had made some friends who helped him land a job back in Washington in Senator J. William Fulbright's office. Clinton felt fortunate to get the job. "I needed a job to go back to Georgetown," he said. "I couldn't afford to pay for it anymore."[4]

College got even a little harder in 1967, when Clinton was twenty-one. Roger Clinton, Sr. learned he was dying of cancer. Every weekend for six weeks Clinton traveled two hundred miles south from Georgetown to the Duke University Hospital in Durham, North Carolina, where his stepfather was being treated.

"I think he knew I was coming down there just because I loved him," Clinton said. "There was nothing else to fight over, nothing else to run from. It was a wonderful time in my life, and I think his."[5] Bill and Roger Clinton managed during those six weeks to reconcile their turbulent relationship, but in the end Bill Clinton had lost another father.

As his years at Georgetown progressed, Clinton's experience in Senator Fulbright's office kept him immersed in the most divisive political issue of the time—the Vietnam War. Senator Fulbright had by now turned against the war, and part of Clinton's job was to read the names, ages, and hometowns of the Americans killed in Vietnam that came over the wire service printer.[6] Clinton was to identify all those from Arkansas so that Senator Fulbright could write a personal letter of condolence to the families. The young men dying in the war now became far more to Bill Clinton than just casualty numbers in the newspaper.

While the war in Vietnam still seemed far away, another event hit closer to home. Riots and fires broke out in many of America's major cities after civil rights leader Dr. Martin Luther King, Jr., was assassinated in Memphis on April 4, 1968. Clinton's high school friend Carolyn Staley was flying into Washington to visit him at Georgetown a short time after the murder.

"I remember flying in and seeing the city on fire," she said. When she met Clinton, she learned he had signed both of them up to drive Red Cross emergency vehicles into the riot area to deliver food.

"They put a red cross on the doors of Bill's white Buick," Staley said, "filled the trunk with the supplies we were to deliver, and gave us each a hat to wear to help cover our face." Later, after delivering the supplies, they parked the car and surveyed some of the damage. "Neither of us said anything as we walked around. We were both numb and shocked at what had happened and what we were seeing."

Staley then expressed to Clinton her wish that she had a camera. "He asked me why I needed a camera. Would I ever forget what I was seeing?"[7]

The shocks of 1968 were not over yet. Only a few weeks after the Martin Luther King, Jr., tragedy, on June 6, 1968, Senator Robert Kennedy was shot dead after his victory speech in the California presidential primary. The Kennedys had been a symbol of hope and political idealism to many Americans, young and old. Now both were gone.

The deaths of both John and Robert Kennedy caused many young people to lose faith in the political system in the late 1960s. For them, the next few years were characterized by despair and a rejection of mainstream values. The hippie culture developed, and many college students turned to drugs such as marijuana and LSD as a way to escape the violence and meaninglessness they saw in society.

Bill Clinton was not part of this counterculture during his Georgetown years, but he identified with their opposition to the Vietnam War. And he had already begun to wonder what the war might mean to his own future. The country seemed to be changing all around him. Since high school and that important day in the White House Rose Garden, he had dreamed of one day entering politics. Now, in the late 1960s, politics had gained a very bad name.

But Bill Clinton stuck to his plan. He would get the best education he could, then someday return to Arkansas in hopes of entering upon a political career in which he could help solve some of the deep problems in his home state.

Late in his college career, Clinton applied for a prestigious Rhodes scholarship to study in Oxford,

Clinton, second from the left, and his friends from Georgetown pose with Roger Clinton Jr., whom Bill had brought to Washington, D.C. for a visit.

England. The process of being awarded the scholarships was very competitive, but several people who knew Clinton's academic record and his accomplishments as a student leader encouraged him to apply.

Clinton asked Senator Fulbright to recommend him to the Rhodes scholarship. Fulbright, who was a former Rhodes scholar himself, was happy to give Bill his enthusiastic recommendation. Clinton still believes Fulbright's support was crucial to his winning the scholarship to Oxford. Bill Clinton was only the second student from Georgetown ever to win a Rhodes scholarship.[8]

Clinton was thrilled to study at the great English university.[9] Because of the scholarship, for the first time he did not have to work while he went to school. He immersed himself in the academic atmosphere at Oxford. A former roommate recalls that Clinton "took full advantage of the fact that he was off on the other side of the Atlantic Ocean, far away from the distractions and preoccupations that had consumed him as a student leader at Georgetown."[10]

"Being in England was incredible," Clinton said. "I got to travel a lot. I got to spend a lot of personal time, learn things, go see things. I read about three hundred books both years I was there.

"For a person like me who just likes to organize every minute of the day—I'm almost compulsively overactive—to have two years where you couldn't do that . . . it was a great deal."[11]

Clinton concentrated on academics while at Oxford but he was not politically inactive. America's involvement in the Vietnam War had grown after January 1968, when the Tet Offensive showed the United States military that the North Vietnamese were capable of staging major attacks on targets all over South Vietnam, including the American Embassy in Saigon. The U.S. counterattack to that offensive involved attacks that killed many innocent civilians. A growing number of people in the United States began to question American involvement, and like a growing number of his friends, Clinton increased his opposition to the war.

He became involved in the anti-war movement both in England and back in Washington during the summer of 1969. He helped organize rallies and protests with the help of an organization called the Vietnam Moratorium Committee. In England these activities were not so much protests as they were organized public forums on issues related to the war and U.S. involvement in the conflict.[12]

It all became quite personal when Clinton received his draft notice. He opposed the war, and clearly he did not want to fight in it. He considered his options while the draft board in Arkansas allowed him to finish his term at Oxford before starting boot camp.

It was a terrible situation. He wanted badly to serve

his country, but not in this war, not in this way. Clinton was opposed to the war, but he was not opposed to the military. So he applied for a Reserve Officer Training Corps (ROTC) scholarship at the University of Arkansas Law School, in hopes that he could serve his country honorably but most likely not be called to fight in Vietnam. The moral dilemmas created by the war, however, were not that simple for Bill Clinton.

Strobe Talbott, a friend of Clinton's from Oxford, and a former senior editor at *Time* magazine, wrote that Clinton "was troubled that while he would be earning an officer's commission and a law degree, some other less privileged kid would have to go in his place and trade bullets with the Viet Cong."[13]

Because of these confusing feelings Clinton changed his mind and canceled his ROTC agreement, putting his name back in the draft. Clinton returned to England and waited to see what would happen. In the draft lottery operative at the time, each eligible young man was assigned a random number, and the lower the number the greater the chance that person would be drafted. On December 1, 1969, Clinton received his lottery number, a high one—311—high enough to almost assure he would never be drafted.

After reconsidering his decision about the ROTC program, Clinton had felt compelled to make himself available to the draft, but he was glad he would not be fighting in a war that he strongly opposed.[14]

The day after he received his draft lottery number, Clinton applied to Yale Law School. He could have had a third year in England on the Rhodes scholarship, but when he was offered a scholarship to attend Yale Law School in the fall of 1970, Bill thought he had to go for the law degree. He returned home to prepare for his studies at Yale.[15]

The 1960s were over, and Clinton had not emerged unscathed by them. But he remained hopeful about the future. Of the 1960s Clinton said, "Even though there was a fair share of pain and disillusionment, there was a great sense of possibility, of hope—a sense that the system could be made to work."[16]

He was anxious to get working on that system, and become a leader in a country that had greatly changed in a very short time.

5

Yale, Hillary, and the First Race

Bill Clinton arrived in New Haven, Connecticut, to attend Yale Law School in the fall of 1970. Even though he had the scholarship, Clinton had to start working again to supplement the cost of his education. He worked as many as three part-time jobs at once. He taught at a local community college and worked for a city councilman in Hartford. Clinton also worked for a lawyer in downtown New Haven who had him investigating civil cases.

"I wound up going into tenements where people were shooting up heroin, doing stuff like that," Clinton said. "I had some interesting jobs."[1]

His hair was longer and his attitudes were more liberal than before he had left for England, but much about him was still the same. He was working hard, learning as much as possible, and always telling people the great things about Arkansas and how he planned to go back there someday.

One afternoon, a young woman passing by Clinton's student lounge overheard him declaring to his friends, "And not only that, we have the largest watermelons in the world!" She asked her friends who he was, and they replied, "Oh, that's Bill Clinton, and all he ever talks about is Arkansas."[2]

Several days later, Clinton and the young woman happened to be seated at opposite ends of a long desk in the Yale Law School Library. A friend was trying to convince Clinton to join the *Yale Law Review*, but Clinton was paying little attention. He kept glancing over his friend's shoulder at the woman behind the books and notepads at the other end of the table.

"She was down at the other end, and . . . I just kept staring at her," Clinton said. "And she closed this book, and she walked all the way down the library . . . and she came up to me and she said, 'Look, if you're going to keep staring at me, and I'm going to keep staring back, I think we should at least know each other.'" For one of the few times in his life, Bill Clinton was at a loss for words.

"I'm Hillary Rodham," she said, "what's your name?"[3] For a moment, Clinton couldn't even remember his name.

"I was so embarrassed," Clinton said. "It turned out

she knew who I was. But I didn't know that at the time. I was real impressed that she did that. And we've been together, more or less, ever since."[4]

Hillary Rodham came from Chicago where her father was a textile manufacturer. She grew up with two brothers in the suburb of Park Ridge, Illinois, before attending Wellesley College, in Massachusetts. During her senior year at Wellesley she was elected president of the student body. She graduated with high honors in 1969.

Hillary Rodham was curious about Clinton's plans to return to Arkansas. "Most of us, including me when I first met him, didn't have any idea what that meant," Hillary said. "We'd never been to Arkansas. We didn't know very much about the state. Frankly, what we knew was colored by 1957 and Orval Faubus."[5]

Orval Faubus was governor of Arkansas in 1957, when nine black students attempted to enter the all-white Central High School in Little Rock. Faubus ordered the Arkansas National Guard to stop the students from entering the school, but President Eisenhower intervened, ordering a U.S. Army division to Little Rock to ensure that the black students were allowed to safely enter the school. Hillary Rodham, like many other Americans, had only heard of Arkansas in terms of this tense chapter in the civil rights movement, which cast the state in a very unpleasant light. Still,

38

Hillary was intrigued with Bill's plans to return there someday.[6]

Don Pogue, Clinton's roommate, remembers Bill and Hillary had well-matched intellects and personalities. "People who think Hillary is smart are like people who think Shakespeare is a good writer," Pogue said. "They are right, but they've missed the point. There is a difference between being good and being very good. Hillary was very good.

"Bill and Hillary really were a good match. She was more Midwestern, schooled in straight, analytical thinking. Bill noticed subtle differences. . . . He wasn't satisfied with just being smart. He would always take his papers back and rewrite them one last time. I remember being frustrated as he noticed shades of gray in what appeared black and white to me, and being impressed by how well he expressed the different hues."[7]

In the summer and fall of 1972, Clinton and Rodham took leave from Yale and moved to Texas to work on the presidential campaign of Senator George McGovern. Clinton was McGovern's state coordinator for Texas, and Rodham worked in San Antonio on registering Hispanic voters for the Democratic National Committee.

For Clinton this was valuable experience in learning how to get votes. Texas was a large and diverse state, and he had to coordinate many different groups of people with many different political perspectives in order to do his job.

Taylor Branch, who worked with Clinton in Texas, said, "Bill was way ahead of me in seeing that a lot of politics had to do with how people got along, and understanding how individuals worked . . . . He knew how to reach people, how to play to their strengths and weakness. Politics is love of people and the process. Bill was naturally good at that."[8]

Clinton had supported McGovern long before he won the Democratic nomination, but he realized long before the election that the McGovern agenda was too liberal and too unstable to appeal to the American people. Clinton said the average person could not identify with McGovern because "this campaign and this man did not have a core, a center, that was common to the great majority of the country."[9]

McGovern lost as incumbent President Richard Nixon won a landslide re-election victory in November of 1972. The campaign had not been successful, but Clinton and Rodham returned to Yale having made some good and politically talented friends who would play important roles in their futures.

Clinton's years at Yale were not all school and politics. It was a period when Clinton had many good times with close friends. They talked about the news, played touch football, and listened to rock music on the stereo. Bill helped out by sometimes cooking for his roommates, but as Don Pogue remembers, Clinton's cooking was not very creative.

"There really isn't much to be said for Bill's cooking," Pogue said. "Basically, Bill is a fryer. He fried everything. And he did it in a continuous motion—from frying pan to plate and into the mouth. All while he was standing there holding the frying pan. But at least he washed the frying pan. That was part of the continuous motion—ending up in the sink. I can see him standing there, metal sponge in hand, still talking, smiling."[10]

Clinton's years at Yale had changed the way he looked at how law fit into society. He had learned how to identify important points in large volumes of case law, how to negotiate, and how to persuade people to his point of view. Yale was known for teaching its law students not only what the law *is*, but what the law *should be*.[11] This was an excellent education for someone like Clinton, who would go on to write his own legislation.

Clinton graduated from Yale Law School in 1973 at the age of twenty-six. Both he and Rodham were immediately offered several positions in Washington. Rodham went to Boston, however, to become an attorney for the Children's Defense Fund, an organization she would remain involved with throughout her legal career. Clinton, as he had always said, planned to return to Arkansas, but he and Rodham would stay in touch.

Clinton's original plan was to borrow some money to set up a private law practice back in Hot Springs. While he was preparing to leave Yale, a professor at the University of Arkansas Law School in Fayetteville contacted him and suggested he apply for two teaching vacancies the school had for professors. Clinton thought about this suggestion while driving home from Yale. He changed his mind about the law practice.

When he reached Arkansas, he pulled into a gas station and made a phone call to the dean of the law school, telling him he wanted the job. The dean told the twenty-six-year-old Clinton that he thought he was too young to teach in law school.

"I've been too young to do everything I've ever done," Clinton replied, and persuaded the dean to give him an interview, which ultimately got him the job.[12]

Clinton taught constitutional law, criminal procedure, and admirality law at the law school in Fayetteville. His students remember Clinton as an interesting and energetic teacher who always had an incredible sense of fairness in the classroom. On the first day of classes, the young professor was often mistaken as a classmate by his students.

In addition to his teaching, Clinton was busy, as always, in the political arena. In early 1974 he began talking among his friends at the law school about finding a candidate to challenge John Paul Hammerschmidt, the Republican congressman for Arkansas' 3rd District, which covered much of northwest Arkansas, including Hot Springs and Fayetteville. Hammerschmidt had never faced a tough race since being elected in 1966. The district was heavily Republican and Clinton knew it would be a tough race for any Democratic candidate. Clinton claims he asked a half dozen of his friends at Fayetteville to make the run for Congress, but they all declined. Although this was much earlier than he had ever planned to run for public office, it occurred to Clinton that he himself was very qualified to go up against Hammerschmidt for the next seat in Congress. He had been teaching only three months when he decided to begin his political career with an uphill congressional race against the incumbent and wealthy John Paul Hammerschmidt.

Clinton remembers the campaign fondly as the "best campaign I ever ran."[13] He climbed into his beat-up 1970 Gremlin and traveled all over the district giving speeches and attending meetings. He gained important financial support from the Arkansas Education Association and the Arkansas AFL-CIO, which represented labor unions in the state. With their financial support, the help of a small campaign staff, and his own hard work, Clinton won the primary election against three other Democrats who had entered the race. Clinton won even though he had been the least known, but few political observers believed he had much of a chance against Hammerschmidt in November.

Two endorsements and a small circle of friends had helped him win the primary, but Clinton was counting on some outside help to beat Hammerschmidt in the general election.

Hammerschmidt had been a vocal supporter of President Richard Nixon and his policies, but in the spring and summer of 1974, the Nixon administration was crumbling as a result of the Watergate scandal. Televised hearings in Washington pieced together for the American public the story of how, during the presidential campaign, Nixon's staff attempted to cover up a burglary attempt at the Democratic National Committee headquarters in the Watergate office complex.

Hillary Rodham left her position with the Children's Defense Fund to accept a position working for the House Judiciary Committee in Washington, D.C., which was investigating the scandal and planning to impeach the President on charges of obstruction of justice, abuse of power, and contempt of Congress.[14]

Clinton knew Nixon's demise could hurt Hammerschmidt. He also knew his own position as a Washington outsider could help him against the incumbent at a time when people were feeling negative toward the government because of Watergate. He would need both of these forces working together to help him win his first political race, an uphill one.

6

The Rising Star

It was after 11 P.M. at a Democratic pre-election dinner in Russellville, Arkansas, when candidate Bill Clinton finally got up to speak. All the candidates for governor, senate, and other offices had spoken. Clinton, who was scheduled to speak last, was only given three minutes on the program. By his turn most of the audience had heard all the speeches they wanted to hear and only wanted to get home. David Pryor, now a U.S. senator from Arkansas, remembers what happened when Clinton got to the podium.

"The crowd was restless, ready to go home," Pryor said. "He got up in those three minutes and immediately mesmerized the audience of several hundred people in a very brilliant three-minute political presentation. He brought the crowd to its feet."[1]

His performance that night caused many Democratic supporters to stand up and take notice of this young newcomer running for Congress. With that short speech, Bill Clinton had arrived on the Arkansas political scene.

The press and media in Arkansas were excited by the young candidate.[2] Clinton was something new and he had a charisma that was beginning to appeal not only to the young, but to the 3rd Congressional District's older voters as well. Through the summer of 1974, Clinton's campaign was shaping up to give Hammerschmidt a real challenge, and the Hammerschmidt people began to take the challenge seriously. They and other past supporters of President Richard Nixon were being hurt at the same time by events in Washington.

Under pressure from the Watergate investigations, President Nixon resigned from office on August 9, 1974. If he had not resigned, he would likely have faced impeachment and conviction. The public's frustration with corruption in government was at an all-time high. Clinton tapped into this frustration, and Hammerschmidt's support of Nixon, and communicated the message that government should be brought back to the people.

Clinton outlined his message at the Arkansas State Democratic Convention in September of 1974. "We ought to go back to the roots of our democracy: the people," he said. "They have some ideas of their own about what the people ought to do.

"In short, the words of a friend of mine who works on the Scott County Road Crew: 'The people want a hand up, not a hand out.'"[3]

With Nixon's resignation, Hillary Rodham's work in Washington for the Judiciary Committee was over. She applied for a job at the law school in Fayetteville so she could be with Clinton. Finally she was in Arkansas. And she loved it.

"It was an adjustment, in the sense that I'd never really lived in the South and I'd never lived in a small town, but I felt so immediately at home," she said.[4] Rodham taught at the law school, ran a legal aid clinic, and coordinated a program that sent students to work with prison inmates. As if she did not have enough to do, she became an unofficial campaign manager for Clinton's run for Congress. Some of Clinton's friends say the campaign was a disorganized experiment until Hillary arrived and began to get things in order.

Clinton's campaign was a real challenge to the wealthy incumbent, but in the end it was not enough. Hammerschmidt won by the narrow margin of 51.5 percent of the vote. Hammerschmidt went back to Washington, but Bill Clinton's life had definitely changed. Even though he had lost, he was considered the "boy wonder" of Arkansas politics. Arkansas newspapers wrote that Clinton was the man to watch, a rising political star.[5]

Clinton and Rodham continued to teach in Fayetteville the next year. The two were not married and did not live together. While Rodham was on a trip to the East Coast to see some old friends, Clinton laid plans to change their living arrangements.

In a very happy mood, Clinton picked Rodham up at the airport on her return. "You know that house you liked?" he asked her. "What house?" she said. During one of their drives through Fayetteville, Hillary had made a passing comment about a little glazed-brick house she thought was pretty. While she was away, Bill had bought it. He'd also furnished the house with an antique bed and flowered sheets. "So you're going to have to marry me," he said as they pulled into the driveway of the house.[6]

Two months later, on October 11, 1975, Bill Clinton and Hillary Rodham were married in a private ceremony for family and friends held at the house. Clinton's brother Roger was his best man. The wedding reception was held at the house the next day and attracted about two hundred friends and supporters from the bride and groom's teaching work and the political campaign.

Clinton's congressional campaign had so impressed the media and other politicians in Arkansas that they were all curious to see what would be his next move. He told his friends at the wedding reception that he planned to run for office again in 1976 but had not decided whether to run against Hammerschmidt again or run for the state attorney general post. Clinton's friend Jim Guy Tucker, a democrat, was the present Arkansas attorney general, but Tucker was planning to vacate the office in order to run for Congress.

Tucker encouraged Clinton to run for attorney general, telling him his impressive law credentials and activist approach to the law would make him a fine attorney general. Clinton gathered his friends around him and once again fielded a strong political campaign. Three Democratic candidates filed to run for the office. When the filing deadline passed in April 1976 with no Republican candidate filing, the three candidates knew that whoever won the primary would essentially win the race.

Clinton handled his two Democratic opponents rather easily, drawing 55 percent of the vote, against their 24 percent and 20 percent, a margin large enough to prevent any need for a runoff election. He then ran unopposed in the 1976 general election, which also elected Jimmy Carter President. In January 1977, Clinton officially became the Arkansas attorney general. He was thirty years old.

During his term as attorney general, Clinton fought against some political trends in Arkansas. Politicians in the Arkansas legislature had long been dominated by the big-money forces of the Arkansas utility companies and business interests. As attorney general, Clinton fought for consumer interests and sought to keep the power and gas utility companies from raising their rates.[7]

He tried to reduce overcrowding in the state's prisons by expanding the work-release program. This program helped prepare inmates for life after their prison sentences were served, and prevented many of them from committing other crimes and returning to prison. He was successful in efforts to curb environmental pollution and he fought to lower electric and telephone rates. This last earned him a reputation as a consumer advocate.[8]

An editorial in the *Arkansas Gazette* said Clinton was "a stout champion of the Arkansas consumer, but, even more importantly . . . a champion of individual rights against arbitrary government."

The *Log Cabin Democrat* speculated on Clinton's future. "He is young and popular, and certainly must be getting a considerable amount of rather flattering encouragement to seek higher office.[9]

Clinton did want to seek higher office, and he was encouraged to do so. Since before he took office as attorney general, he had been setting his sights on becoming governor. Although he had implemented some reforms as attorney general, as governor he hoped to put into motion a whole set of progressive reforms that he had felt—since his high school days in Hot Springs—his state desperately needed.

During his campaign for governor, Clinton told voters that Arkansas' economic problems could only be solved by a commitment to improve the education system in Arkansas. Arkansas could never prosper, he said, as long as it paid its teachers a lower salary than anywhere else in the United States.

Arkansas was, in general, a needy state. Agriculture was still the dominant industry in the state, employing far greater numbers of people than manufacturing and retailing. Arkansas' per capita income in 1975 was just $4,510, forty-ninth out of fifty states in the nation. People in Arkansas have an old saying—"Thank God for Mississippi," which referred to the fact that Arkansas would rank dead last in every economic category if Mississippi did not exist.[10]

In the 1978 primary election, Attorney General Clinton won the Democratic nomination for governor with 60 percent of the vote, carrying 71 out of 75 counties. In the general election his Republican opponent Lynn Lowe, the Arkansas Republican Party's state chairman, accused Clinton of having very liberal views on gun control, marijuana laws, and women's rights, issues that were quite controversial at the time. Lowe used against Clinton the fact that Hillary Rodham had kept her maiden name after marrying Bill, a practice that was considered unusual and improper by many

On January 9, 1979, in the assembly chamber of the Arkansas State House, Bill Clinton was sworn in as the nation's youngest governor. Hillary is at his side holding the Bible for the ceremony.

conservative-minded Arkansans. None of the criticism harmed Clinton, whom the newspapers still cast as Arkansas' rising political star.

Clinton defeated Lowe in the race for governor, winning 338,648 votes to Lowe's 195,550. Clinton was now where he had long wanted to be. He was about to hold the highest political office in Arkansas, and he was ready to bring to it an agenda of education reform, environmental protection, equal opportunity and economic development, and tax relief for the elderly. He was ready to do what he had long been preparing to do. He was ready to change Arkansas.

With Hillary holding the Bible, and with his mother Virginia and brother Roger, Jr. standing nearby, Bill Clinton was sworn in as the fortieth governor of Arkansas on January 9, 1979. At age thirty-two, he was the youngest governor in the nation.

Learning the Hard Way

"I haven't given a lot of thought to being the youngest governor in the country," Clinton said in an interview shortly after taking office in 1979. "I'm trying to be the best, not the youngest."[1]

The new Governor Clinton tried to be the best by going after his agenda for Arkansas like a charging bull. Important to Clinton was keeping his promise to improve education in the state. A major portion of the first legislative session during his governorship was dedicated to budgeting the largest increase of funding for education in the state's history.

Clinton's budget provided a 40 percent increase in elementary and secondary school funding, and a $1,200 salary increase for teachers. Before the salary increase, Arkansas teacher salaries were only two-thirds of the national average. Clinton also tied the legislation to measures that would require students to take mandatory achievement tests, which he said would enable parents, educators, and state officials to make future decisions about education reform.[2]

Clinton's reforms proved to be overambitious. During his two-year term—1979 to 1980—the nation's economy, and thus Arkansas', was sliding into recession. Also, because the Arkansas state constitution did not allow deficit spending, instead living by the rule of a balanced state budget, the state could only spend as much as it took in. Thus, even with the initial support of the state legislature, these two factors—the recession and no deficit spending—created challenges in adequately funding all of the governor's education reform programs, and some could not be implemented.

During his term as governor, Clinton experienced in his personal life something his own father never did—the birth of a child. Chelsea Victoria Clinton was born at Little Rock's Baptist Medical Center on February 27, 1980. It was a moving experience for a man whose father had died before his mother gave birth to him. Hospital workers told reporters that Clinton walked around the area all night holding the baby in his arms.[3]

Continuing in the same working style he had adopted as attorney general, Clinton used his power as governor to fight for consumer interests, defying the powerful utility companies, the Arkansas timber industry, and business interests. Interestingly, no one on the young, idealistic, and inexperienced staff he had brought to his administration apparently realized and warned him that he might be pushing a little too hard and too fast.

His closest advisers became known among legislators as "the bearded wonders" because they had long beards and often wore jeans and T-shirts to meetings. They encouraged Clinton to aggressively attack timber management practices and stop the clear-cutting of so many acres the industry had been doing in the state. Clinton's administration also fought the trucking companies and tried to control public rates charged by the power utilities. All these things perhaps needed to be done, but from a political perspective, Clinton's people were quickly making powerful enemies.

If Clinton was to pass his programs through the state legislature, his administration needed to have the support of legislators. But Clinton's staff was far too abrasive, and soon even the legislature was against him.

"Everybody came in with the new governor, wanting to work with him," said Arkansas State Representative Lloyd George, "but we hadn't got half-way into the session before most of us in the senate and house would like to have impeached him if we could."[4]

"There was a certain arrogance to the first Clinton administration," said Max Brantley, editor of the

Arkansas Times. "They moved way out in front on issues for Arkansas, a very conservative state. They brought in people with far-thinking ideas on rural healthcare, energy conservation . . . all these things ran counter to the business establishment, and they made enemies very quickly."[5]

More trouble was ahead for Governor Clinton. He was under pressure from the highway department and several city and county officials to raise funds for major repairs to the state's highways. He wanted to start the projects but did not want to take funds away from school and health-care programs that he considered essential. Instead, to pay for the road repair projects, Clinton pushed through the legislature a plan to raise fees on car registration tags, and raise the tax on gasoline and tires.

The cost increase for car tags was a shock to people. Everyone in Arkansas had to get car registration tags, and when people stood in the long lines to pay the fees and then learned it would be ten to fifteen dollars more than the year before, they were outraged.

One day Clinton was involved in an angry confrontation at a large factory in southern Arkansas. He was both surprised and confused about what he had seen and heard at the factory.[6]

"They're killing me out there, and they hate my guts," Clinton told his chief of staff, Rudy Moore.

As political problems were mounting late in his first term as governor, Clinton tries to liven up a cabinet meeting before giving them more bad news.

"What are you talking about?" Moore asked the governor.

"It's the car tags," Clinton said.[7]

The fee increase especially hurt the rural poor because the fees were based on the weight of a vehicle, and poorer people usually drove older, heavier vehicles. Everyone who bought their new car tags that year knew that they had young Governor Clinton to blame for the higher fees.

"If I had told people I was going to repeal the car license, I wouldn't have been defeated," Clinton later said. "The fact that I did it, and the fact that I kept telling people 'you gotta like it' struck most people as an act of arrogance."[8]

It got worse. As the time drew near for his campaign for re-election in the spring of 1980, Cuban leader Fidel Castro began allowing some Cubans to leave their country and go to the United States. The Cuban refugees headed for Florida, and the U.S. government had to decide what to do with them. President Carter and the Federal Emergency Management Agency ordered 19,000 of the refugees to be sent to Fort Chaffee, a National Guard and Army Reserve training facility in northwest Arkansas. Because some of the refugees were former inmates of prisons and mental institutions, the government hoped to use Fort Chaffee to process each refugee and determine who should and should not be allowed to stay.

Many of the Cubans were angry that they had not been allowed to stay in Florida and join the large Cuban community there.[9] On May 26, 1980, the day before the primary election, about 350 Cubans rioted and escaped from Fort Chaffee, scattering throughout Sebastian County. Clinton was furious to discover that the federal authorities at Fort Chaffee had done nothing to prevent the Cubans from leaving the base.[10]

At dawn on election day, Clinton sent sixty-five National Guard troops to protect the communities near Fort Chaffee. Two days later the Pentagon sent 150 additional federal troops, but Arkansas state troopers and local police rounded up all the escapees in a few days with no help at all from the federal troops.

Clinton won the primary election with about 69 percent of the vote. But his election troubles were about to begin as the general election campaign commenced. The problems at Fort Chaffee were also far from over. On June 1, less than a week later, nearly 1,000 Cubans charged the gate at Fort Chaffee; again the federal troops did nothing to stop them. About 200 angry refugees ran down Highway 22 toward the small community of Barling, but state troopers managed to stop the refugees and return them to Fort Chaffee.

Clinton decided that was enough. He called the White House and told officials there that they had to give the federal troops the order to use force to keep the refugees on the base. "You can come down here and fix this tonight, right now, or I'm going to call out the entire National Guard and shut the place down," Clinton said. "And I'm not going to let anybody in or out without my approval."[11]

By 4:30 A.M. the next morning, a White House aide had flown to Arkansas and given the federal troops at Fort Chaffee the authority to keep the refugees on the base. Clinton had handled the situation quickly and forcefully, but the political damage had already been done.

Clinton's Republican opponent for governor, Frank White, later ran a television political advertisement showing scenes of the Cubans rioting. The ad blamed Clinton for allowing the refugees to be sent there, even though President Carter had ordered them to Fort Chaffee. Over a three-week period in the early fall, the ad helped shave nineteen points off Clinton's lead in the polls.[12]

White's campaign was also heavily funded by large contributions from the timber industry and the business community, both of which Clinton had alienated with his zeal for protecting consumer interests.

"Bill Clinton fought fiercely against the electric utility to lower electric rates," said Max Brantley. "They didn't like it. And they too spent thousands of dollars trying to elect Frank White.

"The voters of Arkansas were a little bit uncertain about Bill Clinton," Brantley added. "He left them a little nervous. Particularly, he had a wife that didn't take his last name. And these were things that were vaguely unsettling, and when you combine them with some very real political issues—the increase in the car tags, the Cubans rioting—Bill Clinton was ripe to be beaten."[13]

On election day, Bill Clinton, the young rising star, was beaten by some thirty thousand votes. It came as a shock to everyone, including Frank White, because Bill Clinton had been far ahead in the polls as late as mid-October. But as the country's voters swung toward Ronald Reagan in the final days, so did Arkansas.[14]

The period that followed was a time of soul-searching for Clinton. The loss seemed to have derailed a plan he had set for life since he was a teenager. During his farewell address to a packed House chamber, Hillary, holding ten-month-old Chelsea, stood at Bill's side. It was an emotional scene in stark contrast to the day he had confidently taken the oath of office just two years earlier.

Bill Clinton was now the youngest ex-governor in the nation's history.

For the first time in his life Bill Clinton did not know what to do. His success had vanished overnight. He became depressed and often secluded himself. He did not fully understand what had happened and knew even less about what he should do next.[15]

Bill Clinton hugs wife Hillary after his farewell speech to the Arkansas legislature in January 1981. Clinton was now the nation's youngest ex-governor.

Bill went into private law practice with a large firm in Little Rock, the state's capital, but the work did not keep his energies focused. He became careless about his personal life, and rumors began to circulate that he was having an affair with another woman. The rumors made it to the newsrooms, but since Clinton was out of public life, reporters ignored them.[16]

Then, slowly, with the strong support of friends and relatives, Bill came around. He traveled the state, talking to people about what he had done wrong and what he had done right as governor. The newspapers, the public, and Frank White himself, began to realize that White had become governor by accident. He had brought no agenda to the office and had no skill at managing it. Reporters began calling him "Governor Goofy" behind his back.

Soon Bill Clinton was speaking at civic clubs again and being quoted in newspapers criticizing some of White's political decisions. Bill wanted his job back, and he began to believe he could get it. Bill Clinton was rising from the ashes, and he would soon earn himself the name "The Comeback Kid."

8

The Comeback Kid

In defeat, Bill Clinton had learned some important lessons.

"I learned the hard way that you really have to have priorities and make them clear to people," he said. "You have to win people over. And to do that, you have to spend some time listening to them."[1]

Clinton listened. He traveled all over Arkansas, listening to people at Rotary Club luncheons and meeting with small-town newspaper editors. Even during his morning jog in Little Rock he often jogged alongside strangers and asked them what they thought he had done wrong as governor.

About the car tags and other issues Clinton conceded, "A guy who supposedly has an IQ of a zillion did something stupid."[2] He knew the voters had rendered a negative judgment on his term as governor, and he sought to discover from them what he had done wrong. He was determined to learn from his mistakes.

Still, Clinton defied political tradition. Before he even announced he would seek re-election as governor in 1982, Clinton aired a paid television advertisement in February in which he admitted his mistakes and promised he would be more receptive to the ideas and needs of the voters. During the ad, Clinton coined a phrase he would use throughout his campaign: You can't lead without listening.

Growing dissatisfaction with the governorship of Frank White buoyed Clinton's chances of recapturing the office. One of White's most controversial actions was his support for a bill to order schools to teach "Creation Science"—the creation account in the Bible's book of Genesis—in all Arkansas schools. White later admitted he signed the bill without even reading it.

White was also allowing utility rates to rise again, and when news stories revealed he had accepted a free ride in an airplane owned by a utility company, the press accused him of being in league with powerful special interests. A popular bumper sticker started to appear that read, "Don't Blame Me—I Voted for Clinton."[3]

During the ensuing campaign, Hillary Rodham officially changed her name to Hillary Clinton. The *Arkansas Gazette* wrote that Mrs. Clinton was "perhaps a little brisker, a little more outspoken than the traditional

Bill and Hillary Clinton campaigned hard together for his reelection to the Governor's office in 1982. Here Clinton shakes hands amid a crowd of supporters following a speech.

southern governor's lady . . . the name change indicates that she's working at softening her image a bit. . . . And succeeding, apparently. She has become a good hand-shaking campaigner in the traditional Arkansas style."[4]

White painted ex-Governor Clinton as a bleeding-heart liberal who was out of touch with the conservative character of Arkansas. But Clinton blasted back at White for his lack of commitment to education issues. He also attacked White for raising the price of medicine to Medicaid recipients, while giving away $12 million in corporate tax breaks.

From his defeat in 1980, Clinton had learned not to hesitate in firing back hard political volleys at his opponents. During the 1982 campaign he told an audience, "If your opponent picks up a hammer, you need to pick up a meat-ax and cut off his arm."[5] Clinton had been on the receiving end of some rough campaigning in 1980, but by 1982, he had learned that to survive in politics he must also be willing to dish it out.

The 1982 campaign for governor in Arkansas was one of the nastiest in recent memory. When it was over, Clinton had made a dramatic political comeback, winning 54.7 percent of the vote, making him the only governor in the state's history to be defeated and then regain the office.

On election night, Clinton told the crowd at his

Bill Clinton waves in triumph to a crowd gathered to celebrate his reelection victory on election night, November 2, 1982. Clinton said, "I have been given something few people get in life—a second chance."

victory party, "I have been given something few people get in life—a second chance." He intended to make the best of it.[6]

The abrasive staff members—the ones called "the bearded wonders" during Clinton's first term—were gone. No longer would Clinton and his staff tackle an issue simply because they thought it was right and good for the people. Clinton had learned that the people themselves must also truly believe that the government's action is good for them before they will support it, and him.

His new approach to governing was to build a consensus among the voters and the legislature before attacking an issue and trying to bring about change. Throughout the rest of his years as governor, the first and foremost target of this strategy of governing was education reform.

In late September 1983, Governor Clinton went on Arkansas television to address the people about his plans for education. He stated that Arkansas' education system clearly needed more money. "To put it bluntly, we've got to raise taxes to increase our investment in education. Arkansas is dead last in spending per child . . . we have to raise this money for education if we ever hope to get out of the economic backwater of our country."[7]

True to his new style of governing, Clinton appealed directly to the people to support his program before he began work on the legislation. "I ask for your personal

Bill and Hillary Clinton greet supporters outside the assembly chamber of the Arkansas Statehouse following Clinton's swearing-in speech in January 1983.

commitment because it will personally benefit you, your children, your grandchildren and the future of the state we all love so much."[8]

Over several weeks of intensive work, Clinton and state lawmakers worked on the education funding package, which would include salary increases for teachers and improvements in classroom facilities. Tied to the legislation was a rule requiring all Arkansas teachers to take competency tests, which would measure the quality of the state's teachers. Any teacher who did not pass the test would be required to take additional college coursework and retake the test before being allowed to continue teaching in Arkansas.

The Arkansas Education Association (AEA), which had always supported Clinton's education policies, turned strongly against Clinton and the testing requirement.

Despite the teachers' loud protests about testing, Clinton signed the bill into law. Funding to education in Arkansas was increased, and competency tests were now required of all teachers.

Earlier in the year, a new commission had been created to help identify the specific goals of education reform and set new minimum standards for Arkansas schools. The State Board of Education had appointed fifteen members to the new committee. Its choice to chair the committee, with Clinton's encouragement, was Hillary Clinton.

For several months before the new legislation was passed, the committee had held public meetings in all of Arkansas' seventy-five counties, listening to comments from parents, teachers, students, and others with ideas on how the schools could be improved. The recommendations presented by this committee in late 1983 had served as the blueprint for the education reforms targeted in the new legislation. The report also served as the basis for other education reforms throughout Clinton's years as governor. Most educators felt that Hillary Clinton had served well as chair of the committee.[9]

Clinton had asked for support for education reform, solicited the people's suggestions of how it should be done, built consensus among the public and the legislature, monitored the bill's progress through the House and Senate, and then signed the bill into law. With this proven success, Bill Clinton's new style of governing was truly born.

Clinton fought for lower utility rates during his second term. He mediated a legislative dispute between truckers' unions and the highway commission over how to raise more tax revenues for highway repairs. He and his staff also began work on an extensive program to increase Arkansas' industrial development.

Long viewed as a rising star by the Democratic Party, Clinton's stature rose even higher as he was invited to speak during an evening session of the 1984

Democratic National Convention, which nominated Walter Mondale for President. His speech was well received, adding luster to his image and his national political future.

In May 1984, Clinton's family life again took the wind out of his sails and dulled the shine of his success. Clinton learned that his stepbrother, Roger Clinton, Jr., was under investigation for trafficking cocaine. He was also abusing the drug, taking as much as four grams a day. It came as a total shock to Clinton since he had no idea his brother had slid into such dangerous and self-destructive behavior.[10] Although it was very difficult for Clinton, he told the Arkansas state police to go about their jobs and give Roger no special treatment. He was arrested three months later and served a little over a year in a federal prison.

Roger Clinton's drug addiction caused Clinton's memories of his alcoholic stepfather to resurface. The young Bill Clinton had behaved like an adult while he was still a child in an attempt to bring order to the chaos in the family caused by Roger Clinton's alcoholism. Friends remember his mood was very low at the time following Roger, Jr.'s, arrest, because Clinton believed he had failed his family.[11]

He became careless again. Rumors of extramarital affairs were again circulating through the newsrooms, though no evidence was ever found to support them. When Roger, Jr., was released a year later, the Clintons—Bill,

Bill Clinton with four-year-old daughter Chelsea at a Christmas parade in 1984.

Roger, Jr., and their mother Virginia—entered a period of family therapy, which Clinton today claims was very important for all of them.[12]

"I finally realized how my compulsive and obsessive ambition got in the way," Clinton said. "And I think that dealing with that helped me to achieve some better balance."[13]

The issue of his brother's arrest, however, did not harm Clinton as the 1984 election campaign began. He swept to an easy victory in the primary election and defeated his Republican opponent, Woody Freeman, in the general election, with 64 percent of the votes. Arkansas political writer John Robert Starr wrote that "the education issue had made Clinton too strong to handle."[14]

Clinton was inaugurated as governor of Arkansas for the third time in January 1985, at age thirty-eight. He'd risen from defeat to become a strong and shrewd political force in Arkansas, and was increasingly being touted as one of the Democratic Party's most attractive candidate possibilities for the next presidential election.

Throughout the next seven years and two elections, Governor Clinton would continue to work for his policies of education and economic reform in Arkansas. With the advice and encouragement of his many influential friends, he would also begin to flirt seriously with the idea of running for President.

9

The National Figure

Ever since he had been elected Arkansas attorney general back in 1976, the national Democratic Party had viewed Bill Clinton as a strong and hopeful figure in the party's future.

In 1978, shortly after being elected governor, Clinton was asked to moderate a discussion on national health care at the party's national midterm convention. His appearance at the convention, and the excitement over his being elected the youngest governor in the nation, created speculation that he would be tapped as either a running mate for Senator Edward Kennedy or as a new running mate for President Jimmy Carter in the 1980 presidential election.

Clinton had also given a fine speech at the 1984 Democratic National Convention; and he was becoming a leader among fellow governors in the National Governors Association (NGA). In the summer of 1985 he was elected chairman of the Southern Growth Policies Board and Vice Chairman of the NGA. In 1986 he also served as co-chairman of the NGA task force on welfare reform.[1]

Bill Clinton was growing into a national political figure, and when he won re-election to a fourth term as governor of Arkansas in 1986, there was talk that the forty-year-old Clinton would run for President in 1988. Bill would think long and hard about taking that big step.

While he pondered, there was plenty of work for him in Arkansas: preserving the newly implemented school standards, and trying to create more manufacturing jobs in the state. Faced with a state budget shortfall in 1986, Clinton and Arkansas legislators had to rewrite the Arkansas tax code to raise new revenues, and to pass a quarter-cent increase in the sales tax.

Clinton at least had some political room to breathe now in dealing with these matters. Arkansas voters had approved a constitutional amendment in 1984 to extend the governor's term from two years to four years, and Clinton was the first recipient of that extended term. The longer term and a sense of unfinished business at home made the decision about higher office a difficult one for Clinton.

Clinton shares a private moment with Chelsea during the ceremony for his third inauguration as governor of Arkansas in January 1985.

By 1987 there were definite signs Clinton was considering a run for the presidency. He stayed active and visible nationally as Chairman of the National Governors Association, and his comments on national issues appeared in major newspapers and on the TV networks. In February Clinton made a trip to Iowa, the state where, the Arkansas newspapers were quick to point out, the first presidential caucus would be held in 1988.[2]

In April he was invited to the New Hampshire Democratic Committee's quarterly meeting. New Hampshire was another early presidential primary state. When asked about the possibility of running for President, Clinton told reporters he was considering putting a campaign together but had not yet made his decision. Hillary said she would support whatever decision Bill made.

Most news columnists in Arkansas were against Clinton making the run. They felt that he was needed in Arkansas and was still too young and too indecisive to deal with the heavy responsibilities of the presidency.[3] This opinion pointed to what some considered the downside of the governing style Clinton had adopted since his second term as governor. His willingness to negotiate and compromise his proposals in order to get them passed through the legislature was viewed by some as a sign of weakness, or worse, as a lack of principle. But Clinton had always defended his style by explaining he would rather compromise and get half of what he asked for, than not compromise and get nothing.

His speaking engagements in several other states were well received by audiences and the press. It seemed the time might indeed be right for him for President.

On July 15, 1987, Bill Clinton surprised everyone when he announced he would not seek the Democratic nomination for President. "My heart says no," Clinton said at a press conference. He explained that his daughter Chelsea was only seven, and that a presidential campaign would require he and Hillary to be away from her for long periods of time. "That would not be good for her or for us," he said.

"I hope I will have another opportunity to seek the presidency when I can do it and be faithful to my family, my state and my sense of what is right."[4]

Clinton was only forty-one. He would clearly have a shot at running for President, but in 1988 he felt the time was not right for him or his family. He still kept a high profile across the country throughout the primary season, and gave speeches in support of Massachusetts Governor Michael Dukakis, who would eventually win the Democratic presidential nomination. Also that summer, Mayor Andrew Young of Atlanta presented Bill and Hillary Clinton with the National Humanitarian Award from the National Council of Christians and Jews, saying the Clintons' contributions to society represented the best of the South.[5]

Dukakis had more than enough delegates to win the nomination by the time the Democratic National Convention got underway in Atlanta on July 18, 1988. Clinton had garnered a lot of support for Dukakis in the South, so Dukakis asked him to use his well-known speaking talents to make the nominating speech. Clinton had always done well on television, and Dukakis and his advisers were excited about having him deliver the speech on prime-time network television.

Clinton usually spoke from notes or outlines, but this speech was ten pages and would run about fifteen minutes without interruptions. He'd had Dukakis approve the speech, and Dukakis wanted him to deliver all of it.

Clinton stepped to the podium on the evening of July 20, 1988, and *everything* went wrong. The lights in the convention hall did not go down, signaling the delegates to be quiet. They yelled and screamed every time he said Dukakis' name, and he was soon being interrupted by chants of "We Want Mike!" The chants made the speech go longer, and as it dragged on, the delegates became louder and rowdier. Many simply were not listening, and the television cameras caught their disinterest, as well as the fact that Clinton was losing control of the speech and the convention hall.

He appeared nervous and confused, but continued on through the ten-page speech, which now stretched to more than thirty minutes. The only roar of applause came when Clinton said, "In conclusion . . ." The speech was a disaster, and Clinton was the butt of jokes by comedians and newspaper columnists for days after the convention.[6] On *The Tonight Show*, Johnny Carson joked that the surgeon general had just approved Governor Clinton as an over-the-counter sleep aid.

After two days of jokes about Clinton, Carson invited him to appear on the show. A few nights later Bill entered the show's set, laughing, after Carson had given him a long and rambling introduction. As Carson asked Bill how he was doing, Carson set an hourglass on the corner of his desk. Clinton made several jokes about the long speech, and Carson appreciated the governor's good-natured ability to laugh at himself.[7]

Clinton was also prepared to perform a number on his saxophone with Doc Severinson and the orchestra. "Yes, a very . . . short song," he assured Carson. Clinton performed "Summertime" on the saxophone, after which the audience applauded him at length.[8]

The appearance was a great success and salvaged much of his reputation as a magnetic personality. The next night Carson even read a letter on the show in support of Clinton from a Arkansas woman, who also described some of the things she thought made Arkansas great.

In the end, Election Day 1988 turned out better for Clinton than for Michael Dukakis. Dukakis' Republican opponent, Vice President George Bush, thumped him in the election by winning forty states in a landslide victory. Election Day meanwhile brought Clinton something he said had been "a passion of mine for ten years." Arkansas voters approved a new code of ethics for public officials and lobbyists. Clinton said the voters' mandate "is just a big step forward in the quality of government in Arkansas."[9]

Clinton had not given up on taking a big step forward of his own. Despite his performance at the convention, his political stature around the country was still strong. Because of his activities as governor, Clinton was considered an authority on education reform, and in September 1989, he was invited to Charlottesville, Virginia, to take a leadership role in the President's National Education Summit. Clinton co-chaired the meeting and was influential in formulating the conference's six national education goals.

In Arkansas, Bill pushed another round of education reform measures through the legislature. He tightened enforcement of child support laws and fought for policies that would give poor families better health care. He also fought for increased health care and child care for single parents, so that the parent could work during the day.

By 1990 the big question was whether Clinton would seek an unprecedented fifth term as governor. He declared his intention to run again in March 1990. "Even though the fire of an election no longer burns in me," he said, "I decided that I just didn't want to stop doing the job."[10]

Clinton ran against an ex-Democrat named Sheffield Nelson, who tried to convince voters that Clinton's education reforms were not effective and were too expensive. Not enough of them were convinced; Clinton took 57 percent of the vote, his narrowest margin of victory.

Clinton pushed through more reforms in 1991. His new proposals included apprenticeship programs for high school graduates not going to college, a new college scholarship plan, adult literacy programs, an income tax credit for waste reduction and recycling, and scholarships for medical students who promised to set up practices in rural areas.

Clinton's leadership in Arkansas was recognized and admired by other governors. A June 1991 *Newsweek* magazine polled the nation's fifty governors, asking whom among them they felt was the most effective. Thirty-nine percent of them, Democrats and Republicans alike, chose Bill Clinton.[11]

He had the respect of his peers and had managed to remain a national political figure. Now, it was decision time again. The 1992 presidential campaign drew near, and few thought President George Bush could be beaten. Even fewer thought he could be beaten by Governor Bill Clinton.

10

Wild Race for the White House

The U.S. military's performance in the Persian Gulf War in January 1991 sent a wave of patriotism across the country, and with it, a wave of adulation for President George Bush. Bush's management of the crisis, which had put half a million U.S. troops in Saudi Arabia to bring about the liberation of Kuwait from the invading forces of Iraq's Saddam Hussein, ran the public's approval rating of Bush up to 91 percent. His popularity was so high in early 1991 that few potential Democratic presidential contenders were willing to risk what appeared almost certain defeat against him in 1992.[1]

The first Democrat to declare his candidacy was Senator Paul Tsongas of Massachusetts. By the end of the summer the other Democrats included Senator Tom Harkin of Iowa, Virginia state senator Douglas Wilder,

Senator Bob Kerrey of Nebraska, and the mayor of Irvine, California, Larry Agran. Following trips to some early presidential primary states, and dozens of meetings to form a staff and plan a campaign strategy, Clinton decided to run for the presidency.

On October 3, 1991, Governor Bill Clinton declared his candidacy to a large crowd gathered around the steps of Arkansas' Old State House. He characterized the eight years of Ronald Reagan and four years of George Bush as a time when government had ignored the problems of ordinary people, when the gap between the rich and the poor had widened, and our leaders had lost sight of the American Dream.

"The country is headed in the wrong direction fast," he said, "slipping behind, losing our way, and all we have out of Washington is status quo paralysis. No vision, no action, just neglect, selfishness and division."

Clinton insisted it was a time for a fundamental change in America. "The change we must make isn't liberal or conservative. . . . People don't care about idle rhetoric of 'left' and 'right' and 'liberal' and 'conservative' and all the other words that have made our politics a substitute for action. . . . Government's responsibility is to create more opportunity. The people's responsibility is to make the most of it."[2]

Clinton proposed affordable health care for all Americans, a tax system that would make the wealthiest Americans pay their fair share, and apprenticeship programs where students could borrow money for college by paying back a percentage of their income, or through national service.

Bill was now officially on the campaign trail, but no one had any idea how wild the race would become. The nation's economy was slipping into recession, and as it slid deeper, so did George Bush's popularity. This was the chink in Bush's armor—the weak economy—and Clinton planned to make it the main issue of the campaign. It was not hard to sell to the growing number of out-of-work voters.

Clinton's own popularity, however, was nothing to brag about. An early poll of voters in New Hampshire, the first primary state, put Clinton in sixth place among the Democratic candidates. Doing well in the New Hampshire polls was New York Governor Mario Cuomo, a big name in the party, who had not even entered the race. Clinton thought Cuomo would probably enter the race, so he assembled a fine staff of veteran campaigners to help him compete with Cuomo's name recognition and established national reputation.

On December 20, 1991, Cuomo announced that his state's budget woes would prevent him from entering the presidential campaign. A major hurdle to Clinton's progress was gone, but he would need his veteran staff for the surprises ahead.

He had gained momentum in the New Hampshire polls after introducing detailed proposals of how he

Bill Clinton served for twelve years as the governor of Arkansas. He was in the middle of an unprecedented fifth term when he ran for President of the United States in 1992.

would deal with the recession and the national debt. Clinton called his overall plan the New Covenant. He was equal with Paul Tsongas in the polls by the New Year. Throughout January, Clinton pulled slowly ahead, and he appeared for the first time on the cover of *Time* magazine. The January 20 article in *Time* called Clinton "a bold planner but a poor manager," but said, "many Democrats believe he's electable, and that's what they want."[3]

His electability came into serious question just a few days later, when the supermarket tabloid *Star* printed the story of Gennifer Flowers, who claimed she had carried on a twelve-year affair with Clinton. The story forced Clinton to shift all his campaign energy to denying Flowers' story.

It created a somewhat embarrassing media circus. An entire program of ABC's *Nightline* was devoted to the story. Newspapers soon learned Flowers' story was very suspect. She had also lied about such things as receiving a nursing degree and having performed on the *Hee Haw* television show.[4] But the damage to Clinton had already been done. Rumors and jokes about his sexual conduct were flying around the airwaves, in the newspapers, and off every comedian's lips.

Bill and Hillary Clinton hoped to lay the issue to rest by appearing together on the *60 Minutes* television show. During the segment Clinton said he knew Flowers, but denied ever having an affair with her.

When asked if he had ever had an affair, Clinton said he "had caused pain in his marriage" and had acknowledged his imperfection to the American people from the beginning. The Clintons' appearance on the show made the case that they had experienced problems and survived them, and so had their marriage.[5]

It was a strange turn of events after the broadcast. Most of the media now questioned Flowers' story and became sympathetic to Clinton. As he resumed campaigning, he surged ahead in the polls again. Ironically, he now had more name-recognition than the rest of the candidates. When it appeared that he was cruising to victory in the first primary, another question about Clinton's character arose. This time it was about his draft status during the Vietnam War.

The media told and retold the story of how he tried to avoid the draft and then re-entered the draft. His Republican opponents branded him a draft-dodger and questioned how he could be Commander-in-Chief if he had refused to fight for his country. Clinton did not help himself by giving inconsistent answers to questions about the draft. The issue dogged him throughout the campaign, but later polls showed that most Americans did not consider his draft record a significant reason not to vote for him.

The two character issues cost Clinton a win in New Hampshire. His second-place showing was considered a victory, however, in light of all that had happened. He finished second, but once again he was the Comeback Kid. He had now gained momentum, and he managed to carry it through the primary campaign. Other candidates began to run out of money and drop out. Among Democrats, the race was soon between Clinton, Tsongas, and former California Governor Jerry Brown. Republican candidate Pat Buchanan's challenge hurt President Bush by capturing 37 percent of the New Hampshire Republican vote. Worse for Bush, the economy continued to be sluggish.[6]

In March, a petition drive began for independent candidate H. Ross Perot, a Texas billionaire who said he would spend up to $100 million of his own money to get his name on the ballot in fifty states. Perot's unusual candidacy and his often humorous use of one-liners and down-home wisdom captured the media's curiosity. For a while he was ahead of Clinton in the polls.

Clinton's campaign had its ups and downs, though nothing like what had happened in the New Hampshire drive, and by early summer he was poised to go into the Democratic convention with enough delegates to win the nomination. Shortly before the convention Clinton chose Senator Albert Gore, Jr. of Tennessee to be his vice-presidential running mate. Gore, like Clinton, had come of age in the 1960s and was part of the baby boom generation. The two Democrats, in their forties as compared to Bush in his late sixties, gave the Democratic ticket and the election the appearance of a generational change.

The Democratic National Convention that took place in July at New York's Madison Square Garden was a well-orchestrated success for Clinton and the party, which appeared unified behind their centrist candidate. Their good planning was helped by a healthy dose of luck, when Ross Perot quit the race on July 16, only hours before Clinton delivered his acceptance speech. While hammering at Bush on the economy, Clinton invited the Perot people and all those who wanted change to join his campaign.

"When we pull together, America will pull ahead," he told the convention. "We didn't get into this mess overnight, and we won't get out of it overnight. But we can do it . . . reach out and join us in a great new adventure to chart a bold new future."[7]

The convention accomplished its main goal—the country now saw Clinton as presidential. With Perot gone and the convention a success, Clinton zoomed ahead of Bush in the polls. As the Clintons and Gores campaigned on a bus tour through the Midwest, there was now an air of excitement about the campaign; an excitement edged with a sense that, after twelve years, the Democrats could win the White House.

The Republican National Convention in August underlined the party's lack of enthusiasm for George Bush. Bush hurt himself further by allowing his former

Presidential candidate Bill Clinton and his Vice Presidential candidate, Senator Albert Gore from Tennessee, accepted the Democratic Party's nomination at the Democratic National Convention in New York's Madison Square Garden in July 1992.

Republican opponent Pat Buchanan to deliver a convention speech full of bigoted attacks on minorities and homosexuals. The angry speech alienated many moderate Republicans and more conservative Democrats who had voted for Reagan and Bush. Still, Bush's biggest obstacle to re-election was the lagging economy.[8]

The economy continued to look bleak, and Bush had never taken any real action to get it moving again. In fact, it had taken him nearly a year to acknowledge there was a recession. He could not campaign convincingly on his economic plans for a second term. Although the blame for the recession and the changing economic picture around the world could not all be laid on Bush's shoulders, his leadership in domestic affairs throughout his term had seemed detached and disinterested.

While Clinton campaigned on saving the economy and criticizing Bush's record in dealing with it, Bush attacked Clinton as a failed governor of a small state. It didn't work for Bush, and just when the race appeared locked in a slow cruise toward a Clinton victory, Ross Perot re-entered the race in October. It became apparent that Perot had always planned to re-enter. Many of his former supporters felt Perot's planned "October surprise" was the kind of political cynicism Perot had criticized earlier, and they could no longer take him seriously. Nevertheless, the election was now a three-man race.

By evening of Election Day, November 3, 1992, it was clear Bill Clinton would be the next President of the United States. Later that night he gave his victory speech and lead cheers before a huge crowd of supporters gathered in Little Rock, Arkansas.

Perot's humor and candor made him the star of the first presidential debate. Clinton and Bush acted colorless and overrehearsed in comparison, but Clinton had gone face-to-face with the President for the first time and held his own. His lead in the polls held.[9]

The second debate was more interesting. The three candidates took questions from an invited audience of selected uncommitted voters. It was an environment that Clinton thrived in, and that Bush clearly did not. Perot's one-liners grew repetitive, and the debate's open-ended format revealed his poor command of the issues. Clinton's knowledge of the issues and his personal connection with the people in the audience clearly made him the winner of the second debate. The third debate was arguably a draw.

Clinton's lead held through the final days. In an effort to press the electorate for a mandate, Clinton covered 5,000 miles in the last forty-eight hours of the campaign, visiting fourteen cities in seven states. Clinton returned to Little Rock with Hillary and Chelsea on Election Day, when democracy would take its course.

By evening of November 3, 1992, as Americans watched the colors spread across the electoral maps on the TV networks, it became clear that something that had seemed improbable a few months ago, and impossible a year go, had happened. Bill Clinton, the young Governor who had grown up in a small town in a poor state, had become President of the United States.

11

The Biggest Job
in the World

On January 20th, 1993, Bill Clinton became the 42nd President of the United States. Immediately after his inauguration, the immense challenges of being President descended upon him fast and furious. He attacked them with the same high energy and workaholic attitude he had exhibited all his life, but now the problems were bigger and much more complicated. It had been a big move from the Arkansas Governor's Mansion to the White House, and Clinton soon saw that the stakes were much higher now for every decision he made. His first months were a tough adjustment to the biggest job in the world.

He whipped up a storm of controversy on his first day in office when he announced his intention to lift the ban on homosexuals in the military. The next day his nominee for attorney general, Zoë Baird, withdrew her nomination because of questions about her failing to pay taxes for a nanny who was also an illegal alien.[1]

Later, in April, Republicans in the Senate managed to kill Clinton's economic stimulus package, a plan that was important to his overall economic recovery program. Although the Democrats held a majority in both houses of Congress—a tremendous advantage in passing legislation—Clinton was having great trouble getting the many factions of his own party in Congress to support his programs.

Just as he had in Arkansas, Clinton continued to seek several opinions and consult many people on the solutions to problems during his first months in the White House. This led to something the media referred to as the Squish Factor: the impression that he had trouble making up his mind, that he was too anxious to please, too eager to compromise, and too easily rolled.[2] This style of leadership had served him adequately in Arkansas, but the pressures of the Oval Office would require him to find new ways to assert his power and pass his programs in Washington.

Bill Clinton had also not made it easy on himself. He made many promises during his campaign that would be difficult to keep. He said he would strengthen the economy and reform the health care system. He'd also promised to cut the ever-growing federal budget deficit and to take some action in the ethnic conflict in

In 1993 Bill Clinton took on the powers, and the burdens, of the Presidency. His political leadership abilities would now be challenged by the biggest job in the world.

Bosnia. All these goals could only be realized through complicated negotiations and a political consensus that would be difficult to build. Accomplishing these goals would definitely test a President's ability to lead.

Bill Clinton had asked to be tested. In fact, he had worked feverishly for more than a year for the opportunity to be saddled with the immense pressures of the presidency. Now the whole world would see what kind of leader he was.

He had been working up to this challenge all his life. Ever since he was a young man at Hot Springs High School in Arkansas he had wanted to be a leader. And since the day he shook the hand of President John F. Kennedy in the White House Rose Garden, he had dreamed of helping to solve his country's problems by going into politics. He had been a political leader for fifteen years, but now he faced his greatest test of leadership, and his greatest test of himself, by taking on the biggest job in the world.

Whether Bill Clinton and his presidency passes these tests, only history and the voters will tell.

Chronology

1946—Bill Clinton is born in Hope, Arkansas.

1948 —Bill stays with his grandparents while his
-1950 mother, Virginia, goes to school in New
Orleans.

1950—Virginia returns to Hope; meets and marries
Roger Clinton.

1954—Clinton family moves to Hot Springs.

1963—Meets John F. Kennedy at the White House as
part of a Boys' Nation convention.

1964—Graduates from high school; enters Georgetown
University.

1968—Wins Rhodes scholarship to Oxford, England.

1970—Enters Yale Law School; meets Hillary Rodham.

1973—Graduates from Yale; takes law professorship at
law school of the University of Arkansas in
Fayetteville.

1974—Defeated in run for Congress.

1975—Marries Hillary Rodham in Fayetteville.

1976—Elected Arkansas attorney general.

1978—Elected governor of Arkansas.

1980—Defeated by Frank White in bid for re-election
as governor; daughter Chelsea is born.

1982—Re-elected to second term as governor of
Arkansas.

1983—Implements series of education and economic
-1985   reforms in Arkansas.

1990—Re-elected to unprecedented fifth term as
      governor.

1991—Announces candidacy for President in October.

1992—Elected 42nd President of the United States.

Chapter Notes

Chapter 1

1. ABC network telecast of Clinton Inauguration, 1993.

2. Bill Clinton. "Inaugural Address," Washington, D.C., January 20, 1993.

3. Ibid.

4. Bill Clinton, "A Vision for America: A New Covenant," Democratic National Convention, New York City, July 16, 1992.

5. Ibid.

Chapter 2

1. Jim Moore, *Young Man in a Hurry* (Fort Worth, Tex.: The Summit Group, 1992), p. 20.

2. PBS television broadcast of *Frontline*, "The Choice '92," October 29, 1992, produced by the Lennon Documentary Group.

3. Charles F. Allen and Jonathan Portis, *The Life and Career of Bill Clinton: The Comeback Kid* (New York: Carol Publishing Group, 1992), p. 5.

4. *Frontline* broadcast.

5. Robert Levin, *Bill Clinton: The Inside Story* (New York: Shapolsky Publishers, 1992), p. 11.

6. Moore, p. 23.

7. Levin, p. 13.

8. Allen and Portis, p. 13.

9. *Frontline* broadcast.

10. Allen and Portis, p. 13.

11. Judith Warner, *Hillary Clinton: The Inside Story* (New York: Signet, 1993), p. 48.

12. Moore, p. 26.

Chapter 3

1. Charles F. Allen and Jonathan Portis, *The Life and Career of Bill Clinton: The Comeback Kid* (New York: Carol Publishing Group, 1992), p. 18.

2. Jim Moore, *Young Man in a Hurry* (Fort Worth, Tex.: The Summit Group, 1992), pp. 23–25.

3. Robert E. Levin, *Bill Clinton: The Inside Story* (New York: Shapolsky Publishers, 1992), pp. 30–31.

4. Ibid., p. 31.

5. Gail Sheehy, "What Hillary Wants," *Vanity Fair*, May 1992, p. 214.

6. Howard Fineman and Ann McDaniel, "You Didn't Reveal Your Pain," *Newsweek*, March 30, 1992, p. 37.

7. Allen and Portis, pp. 15–16.

8. Matthew Cooper, "Bill Clinton's Hidden Life," *U.S. News and World Report*, July 20, 1992, p. 30.

9. Levin, p. 40.

10. PBS television broadcast of *Frontline*, "The Choice '92," October 29, 1992, produced by the Lennon Documentary Group.

11. Cooper, p. 30.

Chapter 4

1. Matthew Cooper, "Bill Clinton's Hidden Life," *U.S. News and World Report*, July 20, 1992, p. 31.

2. Robert E. Levin, *Bill Clinton: The Inside Story* (New York: Shapolsky Publishers, 1992), p. 42.

3. Charles F. Allen and Jonathan Portis, *The Life and Career of Bill Clinton: The Comeback Kid* (New York: Carol Publishing Group, 1992), p. 23.

4. Ibid.

5. Peter Applebome, "Bill Clinton's Uncertain Journey," *New York Times Magazine*, March 8, 1992, p. 60.

6. Howard Fineman, "60s Coming of Age," *Newsweek*, July 20, 1992, p. 34.

7. Carolyn Staley, interview with the author, May 18, 1993.

8. Jim Moore, *Young Man in a Hurry* (Fort Worth, Tex.: The Summit Group, 1992), pp. 31–33.

9. Allen and Portis, p. 30.

10. Ibid, p. 30.

11. Ibid, p. 31.

12. Strobe Talbott, "America Abroad," *Time*, March 9, 1992, p. 38.

13. Ibid.

14. Levin, pp. 80–84.

15. Fineman, p. 35.

16. Cooper, p. 31.

Chapter 5

1. Charles F. Allen and Jonathan Portis, *The Life and Career of Bill Clinton: The Comeback Kid* (New York: Carol Publishing Group, 1992), p. 32.

2. Judith Warner, *Hillary Clinton: The Inside Story* (New York: Signet, 1993), p. 47.

3. Gail Sheehy, "What Hillary Wants," *Vanity Fair*, May 1992, p. 215.

4. Robert E. Levin, *Bill Clinton: The Inside Story* (New York: Shapolsky Publishers, 1992), p. 91.

5. Allen and Portis, p. 34.

6. Warner, p. 58.

7. Levin, p. 93.

8. Ibid., p. 94.

9. David Broder, *The Changing of the Guard: Power and Leadership in America* (New York: Penguin Books, 1981), p. 381.

10. Levin, pp. 87–88.

11. Warner, pp. 43–46.

12. Allen and Portis, p. 38.

13. Peter Applebome, "Bill Clinton's Uncertain Journey," *New York Times Magazine*, March 8, 1992, p. 26.

14. Gary Wills, "Beginning of the Road," *Time*, July 20, 1992, p. 57.

Chapter 6

1. Robert E. Levin, *Bill Clinton: The Inside Story* (New York: Shapolsky Publishers, 1992), p. 108.

2. Charles F. Allen and Jonathan Portis, *The Life and Career of Bill Clinton: The Comeback Kid* (New York: Carol Publishing Group, 1992), p. 47.

3. Text of speech delivered at Arkansas State Democratic Convention, Hot Springs, Arkansas, September 13, 1974.

4. Gail Sheehy, "What Hillary Wants," *Vanity Fair,* May 1992, po. 215.

5. David Osborne, *Laboratories of Democracy* (Boston: Harvard Business School Press, 1988), p. 87.

6. Sheehy, p. 215.

7. Osborne, p. 87.

8. "Bill Clinton," *Current Biography Yearbook, 1988* (New York: H.W. Wilson Company), p. 119.

9. Levin, p. 121.

10. Judith Warner, *Hillary Clinton: The Inside Story* (New York: Signet, 1993), pp. 79–80.

Chapter 7

1. PBS television braodcast of *Frontline,* "The Choice '92," October, 29, 1992, produced by the Lennon Documentary Group.

2. Phyllis Finton Johnston, *Bill Clinton's Public Policy for Arkansas: 1979–1980* (Little Rock, Ark.: August House, 1982), pp. 13–28.

3. Judith Warner, *Hillary Clinton: The Inside Story (New York: Signet, 1993), pp. 103–104.*

4. *Frontline* broadcast.

5. Maria Henson, "Clinton Says He's Learned From Past," *Arkansas Gazette,* May 18, 1986, p. 1A.

6. *Frontline* broadcast.

7. Ibid.

8. Ibid.

9. Phyllis Finton Johnston, pp. 79–80.

10. Ibid, pp. 72–75.

11. Ibid., p. 75.

12. *Frontline* broadcast.

13. Ibid.

14. Robert Johnston, "1980 Election in Arkansas," *Arkansas Political Science Association,* February 1981, p. 3.

15. Warner, p. 109.

16. Ibid., pp. 110–112.

Chapter 8

1. Matthew Cooper, "Bill Clinton's Hidden Life," *U.S. News and World Report,* July 20, 1992, p. 30.

2. Ibid., p. 33.

3. Robert Levin, *Bill Clinton: The Inside Story* (New York: Shapolsky Publishers, 1992), p. 147.

4. Judith Warner, *Hillary Clinton: The Inside Story* (New York: Signet, 1993), p. 117.

5. Jim Nichols, "'Learn From GOP's Victory,' Clinton Urges Florida Party," *Arkansas Gazette,* October 11, 1981, p. 1A.

6. PBS television broadcast of *Frontline,* "The Choice '92," October 29, 1992, produced by the Lennon Documentary Group.

7. Text from televised address delivered September 27, 1983.

8. Ibid.

9. Warner, pp. 129–132.

10. Levin, p. 164.

11. Levin, p. 166.

12. Peter Applebome, "Bill Clinton's Uncertain Journey," *New York Times Magazine,* March 8, 1992, p. 63.

13. Ibid.

14. John Robert Starr, *Yellow Dogs and Dark Horses* (Little Rock, Ark.: August House, 1987), p. 83.

Chapter 9

1. "Bill Clinton," *Current Biography Yearbook, 1988* (New York: H.W. Wilson Company), p. 121.

2. Charles F. Allen and Jonathan Portis, *The Life and Career of Bill Clinton: The Comeback Kid* (New York: Carol Publishing Group, 1992), p. 117.

3. Ibid., p. 119.

4. Ibid., p. 123.

5. Judith Warner, *Hillary Clinton: The Inside Story* (New York: Signet, 1993), p. 151.

6. *Current Biography Yearbook, 1988,* p. 122.

7. PBS television broadcast of *Frontline*, "The Choice '92," October 29, 1992, produced by the Lennon Documentary Group.

8. Ibid.

9. Jim Moore, *Young Man in a Hurry* (Fort Worth, Tex.: The Summit Group, 1992), pp. 144–145.

10. Robert E. Levin, *Bill Clinton: The Inside Story* (New York: Shapolsky Publishers, 1992), p. 180.

11. "Ranking the Governors," *Newsweek*, July 1, 1991, p. 27.

Chapter 10

1. George J. Church, "The Long Road," *Time*, November 2, 1992, p. 29.

2. Governor Bill Clinton, Announcement of Candidacy for President; Old State House, Little Rock, Arkansas, October 3, 1991.

3. George J. Church, "Is Bill Clinton for Real?" *Time*, January 20, 1992, p. 15.

4. Charles F. Allen and Jonathan Portis, *The Life and Career of Bill Clinton: The Comeback Kid* (New York: Carol Publishing Group, 1992), pp. 188–189.

5. Ibid., pp. 190–192.

6. Lance Morrow, "The Torch Is Passed," *Time*, January 4, 1993, p. 24.

7. Governor Bill Clinton, "A Vision for America: A New Covenant," Democratic National Convention, New York City, July 16, 1992.

8. Morrow, p. 24.

9. Howard Fineman, "Face to Face to Face," *Newsweek*, October 19, 1992, pp. 20–24.

Chapter 11

1. Nancy Gibbs, "Thumbs Down," *Time*, February 1, 1993, pp. 27–29.

2. Joe Klein, "Slow Motion," *Newsweek*, May 24, 1993, pp. 16–17.

Further Reading

Allen, Charles F. and Portis, Jonathan. *The Life and Career of Bill Clinton: The Comeback Kid.* New York: Carol Publishing Group, 1992.

Applebome, Peter. "Bill Clinton's Uncertain Journey." *New York Times Magazine*, March 8, 1992.

Cooper, Matthew. "Bill Clinton's Hidden Life." *U.S. News and World Report*, July 20, 1992.

Fineman, Howard. "60s Coming of Age." *Newsweek*, July 20, 1992.

Levin, Robert E. and Barbara, James D. *Bill Clinton: The Inside Story.* New York: Shapolsky Publishers, 1992.

Martin, Gene L. and Boyd, Aaron. *Bill Clinton: President From Arkansas.* Greensboro, N.C.: Tudor Publications, 1993.

Moore, Jim. *Clinton: Young Man in a Hurry.* (Fort Worth, Tex.: The Summit Group, 1992.

Morrow, Lance. "The Torch Is Passed." *Time*, January 4, 1993.

Warner, Judith. *Hillary Clinton: The Inside Story.* New York: Penguin Books, 1993.

Wills, Gary. "Beginning of the Road." *Time*, July 20, 1992.

Index